T0007864

WILL
THE CIVIL ENGINEER

A City Infrastructure Story

by Chadd Kahlsdorf, P.E., PMP
Illustrated by Lime Valley Advertising, Inc.

Real People. Real Solutions.

Esri Press
REDLANDS | CALIFORNIA

This is Will. His dad uses funny words when he talks about his job. Words like **structure**, **utilities**, and **specifications**.

One day Will asked his dad what he's talking about.

Will's dad said, "I am a **civil engineer** and do lots of different things. I use math and science to make the world a better place."

I can tell by the look on your face you are not sure what that means. Well, let me explain, everything that is built has an engineer.

Civil engineering is a job that has been around a very long time. Without it, the world would be very different than it is today.

You might have heard of the Great Wall of China and the pyramids in Egypt.

But have you heard of the Golden Gate Bridge and the Hoover Dam?

They are all works of engineers that stand the test of time and show us how long things can last when they're built right.

The water is pulled from a well or a river. The water goes to a building called a **treatment plant**, where it is cleaned and sent through pipes under the street and into our house.

Engineers build **booster stations** to make sure there is enough water pressure for everyone to use the water at the same time.

Civil engineers design each step of the **water system**.

Do you know what happens to the water that goes down the drain or when the toilet is flushed?

All the water with all its gunk is collected in underground pipes and sent to be cleaned before it goes back to a river or well.

This, too, is all designed by civil engineers.

You know the roads we take to the grocery store and to school?

They are all designed by civil engineers to make sure the pavement is strong enough and the roads are wide enough for all the cars and bikes.

Civil engineers design the roadway markings, traffic lights, and signs.

Civil engineers make sure they are in the right place to help drivers be safe and do the right thing at the right time.

Remember when we flew to see your uncle?

A civil engineer designed the **runways** so airplanes move safely from the air to the ground.

Civil engineers also make sure landing approaches are safe and not too close to buildings, trees, or towers.

Civil engineers design all types of structures from bridges over water...

...to buildings of all sizes...

...to deep tunnels for utilities.

Civil engineers also design walls to hold back hills and mountains so there can be flat ground to use for other things.

Civil engineers work to protect lakes, rivers, and streams so we can go fishing and swimming.

We help clean up environmental messes left behind and design dumps so trash stays in one place.

This helps humans, plants, and animals be healthy.

Civil engineers work in the community to find problems that need to be solved.

They think of a solution and create construction drawings and specifications for it.

Then civil engineers give the plans to construction workers and supervise them to make sure the solution is built right.

Will had one more question to ask, "Dad, do you think I can be a civil engineer, too?"
Will's dad smiled and said, "Of course you can, Son."

If you want to be an engineer, it takes hard work.

You will need to study math and learn science and other skills, too.

If you like to solve puzzles and don't mind hard work, then the men and women who are engineers want you to be an engineer, too!

Glossary

Booster Station — A pump system that is used to increase water pressure so our homes and businesses have a nice flow of water out of the faucets and showerheads.

Civil Engineer — A person that uses math, science, and other tools to design, build, and maintain buildings, roads, facilities, and more.

Runway — A flat strip of smooth pavement where airplanes take off and land.

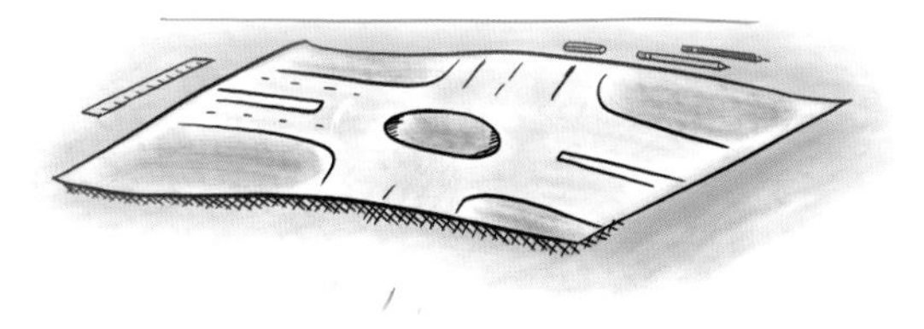

Specifications — A manual that includes design details, a list of materials, and other special instructions to help a contractor build a project.

Structure — An object built from pieces, like buildings, bridges, tunnels, dams, etc.

Treatment Plant — A building that contains equipment and tanks used to clean the water. With the removal of dirty materials, the water can be drunk or released into the environment.

Utilities — Services used by people, including electricity, gas, water, sewers, and internet.

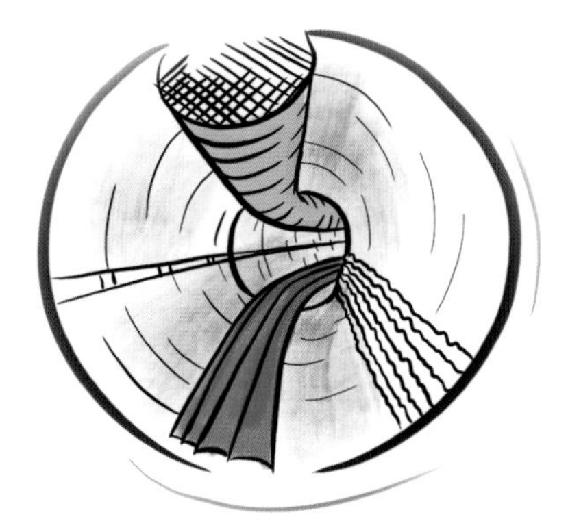

Water System — Infrastructure for collecting, transmitting, treating, storing, and distributing water for a community.

Also available from
STEAM at Work!

Learn more at go.esri.com/willlovesbuilding.